Table of Contents

Master Builders

Do you know the story of the three little pigs? Each little pig built a house. One was made out of straw, another out of sticks, and the third out of bricks.

Beavers are well-known animal architects. They build dams out of sticks and mud. Their homes, called lodges, are inside the dams.

LEVEL
3

Animal Architects

Libby Romero

NATIONAL
GEOGRAPHIC

Washington, D.C.

For Katrina —L. R.

Published by National Geographic Partners, LLC, Washington, D.C. 20036.

Designed by Yay! Design

Library of Congress Cataloging-in-Publication Data

Names: Romero, Libby, author.
Title: Animal architects / by Libby Romero.
Description: Washington, DC : National Geographic Kids, [2019] | Series: National geographic readers | Audience: Ages 6-9. | Audience: K to grade 3.
Identifiers: LCCN 2018031443 (print) | LCCN 2018032652 (ebook) | ISBN 9781426333293 (e-book) | ISBN 9781426333309 (e-book + audio) | ISBN 9781426333279 (pbk.) | ISBN 9781426333286 (hardcover)
Subjects: LCSH: Animals--Habitations--Juvenile literature.
Classification: LCC QL756 (ebook) | LCC QL756 .R66 2019 (print) | DDC 591.56/4--dc23
LC record available at https://lccn.loc.gov/2018031443

The author and publisher gratefully acknowledge the expert content review of this book by Jason Matthews, master naturalist and environmental educator, Montana Natural History Center, and the literacy review of this book by Mariam Jean Dreher, professor of reading education, University of Maryland, College Park.

Photo Credits

AL = Alamy; GI = Getty Images; MP = Minden Pictures; NGC = National Geographic Creative; SS = Shutterstock

Cover, Danita Delimont/GI; header (throughout), super-granhero/SS; vocab (throughout), Lana_Samcorp/SS; 1, Grafissimo/GI; 3, Eric Isselée/GlobalP/GI; 4-5, Arterra/UIG via GI; 4, Tom & Pat Leeson/ARDEA; 6, Michael Potter11/SS; 7 (LE), Maresa Pryor/NGC; 7 (RT), imageBROKER/AL; 8, Panoramic Images/GI; 9, Thilanka Perera/GI; 10, Konrad Wothe/MP; 11, Tim Laman/NGC; 12, Christopher Murray/EyeEm/GI; 13, Don Bartletti/Los Angeles Times via GI; 14, Federico.Crovetto/SS; 15, Perennou Nuridsany/Science Source; 16, Dr. Gonzalo Giribet/NGC; 17 (UP), Genevieve Vallee/AL; 17 (LO), Pong Wira/SS; 18, thatreec/GI; 19, Mark W. Moffett/NGC; 20, Jason Edwards/NGC; 21, DeAgostini/GI; 22, muendo/GI; 23 (LE), Juergen Freund/AL; 23 (RT), Pan Xunbin/SS; 24, Albert Krebs/Entomologie/Botanik, ETH Zürich; 25, Dr. Jerome G. Rozen; 26, Maslov Dmitry/SS; 27, StudioSmart/SS; 28, Alfred Trunk/McPhoto/ullstein bild via GI; 29, Carson Baldwin Jr./Animals Animals; 30 (1), Jason Edwards/NGC; 30 (2), John Porter LRPS/AL; 30 (3), DigitalGlobe via Getty; 31 (4), Tim Laman/NGC; 31 (5), Konrad Wothe/MP; 31 (6), Michael Poliza/NGC; 32 (UP), Ingo Arndt/MP; 32 (CTR LE), Roman Bodnarchuk/SS; 32 (CTR RT), Elif Bea/SS; 32 (LO), mahmood alishahi/SS; 33, George Grall/NGC; 34 (UP), Darlyne A. Murawski/NGC; 34 (LO), Al Petteway & Amy White/NGC; 35, George Grall/NGC; 36-37, Andrew Watson/GI; 36, Tim Laman/NGC; 37, Ryan Rossotto/NGC; 38 (UP), Paulo Oliveira/AL; 38 (LO), Yoji Okata/MP; 39, David Doubilet/NGC; 40-41, Romeo Gacad/AFP/GI; 40, Hugo Van Lawick/NGC; 42-43, Nicky Bay Photography; 43, Ingo Arndt/Nature Picture Library; 44 (1), Kris Wiktor/SS; 44 (2), Chris Mole/SS; 44 (3), Mark W. Moffett/NGC; 45 (4), Ashley Whitworth/AL; 45 (5), brandtbolding/GI; 45 (6), Enrique Lopez-Tapia/Nature Picture Library; 45 (7), Claude Nuridsany & Marie Perennou/Science Source; 46 (UP), StockLite/SS; 46 (CTR LE), Ivan Smuk/SS; 46 (CTR RT), Andrew Watson/GI; 46 (LO LE), Apisit Wilaijit/SS; 46 (LO RT), Sergey Lavrentev/SS; 47 (UP LE), Claude Nuridsany & Marie Perennou/Science Source; 47 (UP RT), Oqbas/SS; 47 (CTR LE), Rosa Baik/EyeEm/GI; 47 (CTR RT), Genevieve Vallee/AL; 47 (LO LE), Yegor Larin/SS

National Geographic supports K–12 educators with ELA Common Core Resources.
Visit natgeoed.org/commoncore for more information.

Printed in the United States of America
18/WOR/1

Pigs don't really build houses, but many animals do build their own homes. Animals build other things, too. They are gifted architects (ARK–ih–tekts). And sometimes, the results are amazing.

Word to Know

ARCHITECT: The designer or creator of something, usually a structure like a building or a bridge

Busy Birds

You've probably seen a bird's nest. But have you seen a nest as big as a haystack? You could in South Africa.

Up to 400 birds can live in a sociable weaver's nest. Other types of birds often move in to share the space.

A sociable weaver perches at an entrance to the nest.

Sociable (SOH–shuh–bull) weavers build huge drooping nests over the tops of trees and telephone poles. The birds build the roof and frame out of large sticks. They use dry grasses to make dozens of rooms. For comfort, they line the rooms with soft grasses and other materials. Finally, they arm each entrance with sharp, spiky straw. This keeps animals that hunt birds, like snakes, out of the nest.

Red ovenbirds are master sculptors. After it rains, the birds shape bits of mud and clay into dome-shaped nests. Inside the nest, there is a back room. A mother lays eggs there. This makes it easier to protect the eggs from predators.

Words to Know

PREDATOR: An animal that hunts and eats other animals

COLONY: A group of one kind of plant or animal that lives together

The red ovenbird gets its name from its nest, which looks like a clay oven.

The baya weaver is another artist. This bird is a master weaver. The male collects long strands of leaves and grasses. Then he weaves and knots them together. Often, several males build nests close together to form a colony.

Baya weavers often build nests that hang from thorny trees or tall palm trees.

9

The male bowerbird builds fancy displays to attract a mate. But the female builds a nest to lay eggs and raise the chicks.

Some birds are master builders. Others are great artists. Male bowerbirds are both.

To attract a mate, male bowerbirds build bowers, or shelters, out of sticks. Then they decorate the front. Some bowerbirds use natural items, such as rocks, moss, nuts, beetles, feathers, shells, or flower petals. Others use colorful or shiny human-made objects. And if none of that works, the male's singing and dancing might do the trick.

bowerbird

Spinning Spiders

Grass spiders spin funnel webs. When prey gets near the opening, the spider darts out and grabs it.

You don't have to look far to see the work of spiders. These animals build their silky webs just about everywhere. Cobwebs might hang in corners in your home. Webs with funnel-shaped tunnels cover grasses and shrubs.

Some of the most beautiful spiderwebs are orbs. They hang between the leaves on plants and trees. Orb webs have rows of circles connected by lines. When the silky threads move, spiders know that predators or prey are nearby.

orb web

Words to Know

ORB: Circular or shaped like a globe

PREY: An animal that is hunted and eaten by another animal

feather-legged lace weaver

Most spiders add sticky glue to their webs to trap prey. But not the feather-legged lace weaver. It uses static cling!

This spider's tiny spinnerets make super-thin silk. The spider yanks the silk from its body and combs it with hairs on its back legs as it builds the web.

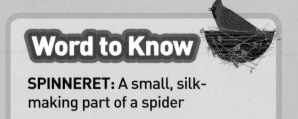

Word to Know

SPINNERET: A small, silk-making part of a spider

This creates an electrostatic charge. The charge attracts insects. It makes them cling to the web, just like socks sometimes stick to towels in a dryer.

How Do Spiders Make Webs?

Spiders pull silk threads out of special body parts called spinnerets. Then they spin webs with their legs. Each set of spinnerets makes a different type of silk—sticky, not sticky, or even superfine. This allows a spider to spin different types of webs.

The net-casting spider doesn't attract prey to its web. It takes the web to its prey. This spider holds its web as it hangs from a silk thread. When prey approaches, the spider throws the net down on its prey.

A net-casting spider's thick, rectangular web is about the size of a postage stamp.

Trapdoor spiders line the inside of their tunnels with silk.

When the trapdoor is closed, plants and soil make the spider's home hard to see.

Not all spiders spin webs. The trapdoor spider digs a tunnel. The door of the tunnel has a silk hinge. The spider closes the door and waits. If an insect gets close, the spider jumps out, grabs it, and drags it into the tunnel.

Ants and Termites

Many ants work together
to pull a leaf into place.

Australian weaver ants use their larvae like glue guns.

Ants live just about everywhere. Australian weaver ants live on bushes and trees. They build nests out of leaves. Working as a team, the ants pull and bend leaves into a tent-like shape. Then the ants pick up their larvae (LAR-vee). The larvae squirt out silk that will glue the nest together.

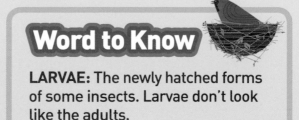

Word to Know

LARVAE: The newly hatched forms of some insects. Larvae don't look like the adults.

anthill

You've probably seen an anthill. Ants don't live in anthills. They live under them in an underground nest. The anthill is just the pile of dirt and sand that the ant colony removed when it built the nest.

These nests are like underground cities. They have lots of rooms connected by tunnels. Each room has a purpose. There are rooms for laying eggs, raising the young, and storing garbage. Leafcutter ants even have a room to grow their own food.

Millions of leafcutter ants cut and carry pieces of leaves to an underground colony. This illustration shows the many tunnels and rooms underground.

Cathedral termite mounds can be more than 15 feet tall and up to 100 years old.

Many termites live underground. But some are famous for the mounds they build aboveground. Cathedral termites make their mounds out of mud, chewed wood, and their own spit and poop.

Compass termites build tall, thin mounds. Each mound points north. Scientists think termites build them this way to control the temperature of their homes. In the morning, the sun shines on the wide eastern side of the mound. Termites go there to warm up. At noon, when the sun is strongest, it only shines on the narrow top. The rest of the mound stays cool.

termite

Compass termite mounds look like wedges that point north.

Bees and Wasps

A female mason bee bites off flower petals to build her nest.

Mason bees live by themselves.
So females build nests on their own.
There are many kinds of mason bees.
A few make special nests out of
flower petals.

First, the mother bee digs a tube-shaped hole in the ground. Next, she lines the hole with flower petals and mud. She fills part of the hole with pollen and nectar. Then she lays an egg on top. To keep the egg safe, she folds over the flower petals and caps the hole with mud.

The nest is built with flower petals on the outside. Inside is a layer of mud and more flower petals.

Each nest holds one egg.

Words to Know

POLLEN: A yellow powder made by flowers

NECTAR: The sweet, sticky liquid formed in flowers

You're probably familiar with honeybees. They live in hives. Honeybees don't build the outside of their hives. They move into human-made beehives or hollow trees. But they do build everything on the inside.

Thousands of bees can live in a beehive.

Are You Smarter Than a Honeybee?

How would you design a home that doesn't waste any space? Ask a honeybee! The honeycomb they make has cells on both sides. The six-sided cells fit together perfectly. This design gives them the most space for growing eggs and storing honey and pollen. It also uses the least amount of wax to create.

The inside of a hive is filled with sheets of six-sided waxy cells. The sheets are called honeycomb. Worker bees make the wax and chew it until it's soft. Then they shape it into honeycomb.

Paper wasps add more cells as the colony grows. One nest can have up to 200 cells.

Paper wasps build nests with six-sided cells, too. To make their papery nests, the wasps chew up pieces of wood and plants. You might have seen their umbrella-shaped nests. They often hang under doorframes or behind window shutters.

Q What did the bees say to the wasp when it tried to enter their hive?

A "Buzz off."

Organ pipe mud daubers build nests out of mud. The female wasp takes a mouthful of mud and forms it into a ball. She carries the mud balls back to a wall. Then she spreads them into long, thin strips to make a nest.

an organ pipe mud dauber building a nest

weird but true!

The organ pipe mud dauber stings a few spiders as she's building a nest. She stuffs them inside the cells so her young can have dinner after they hatch.

29

6 COOL FACTS
About Animal Architects

1 Spider silk is stronger than steel and super stretchy. Recently, scientists made artificial spider silk in labs. It could be used to make everything from artificial limbs to stronger bike helmets.

2 The Darwin's bark spider spins the biggest, strongest webs in the world. Webs can be up to 82 feet wide—as long as two buses!

3 A beaver dam found in Canada was 2,788 feet long. It was so big, it could be seen from space!

Some bowerbirds "paint" the walls of their towers with a mixture of charcoal dust, spit, and plant juices. They use their beaks (like in this photo) or pieces of bark as a paintbrush.

4

5

Swiftlets are small birds that live in caves. They build their nests mostly out of their own spit. People eat their nests in bird's nest soup.

Great apes usually build a new nest each night. Sometimes, the new nest is right next to an old one.

6

Room to Grow

Most caddisfly larvae hang on to their cases with hooked legs and drag them around.

Caddisflies (KAD-diss-flies) are moth-like insects. Their soft, squishy larvae live in the water. To protect themselves, some larvae spin silk cases around their bodies. Others collect nearby objects and build their own suits of armor.

Weird but true!

A French artist wanted to see what caddisfly larvae could do with gold and precious jewels. The larvae built beautiful and expensive works of art!

Bagworm moth larvae do the same thing on land. Each species of bagworm moth makes its own special case. Some look like pinecones or little log cabins.

As bagworm larvae grow, they add more pieces to make their cases bigger.

As a spittlebug nymph grows, it breathes the air inside large bubbles and at the surface of the foam.

a spittlebug blowing bubbles

Spittlebug nymphs don't need to collect things around them. They grow in a pile of foamy spit that they make themselves.

Right after a spittlebug nymph hatches, it makes a sticky liquid. Then it starts to blow bubbles. The bubbly foam covers the nymph's body. It protects the nymph from heat and cold. It also keeps the nymph moist as it grows into an adult.

spittlebug

Word to Know

NYMPH: A newly hatched insect that looks like a tiny adult

Ocean Architects

Some of the greatest animal architects are corals. Corals are tiny animals that live in warm ocean waters. Individual corals, called polyps (POL-ips), are usually less than half an inch across.

The largest coral reef is the Great Barrier Reef in Australia. It stretches 16,000 miles and can be seen from space.

polyps

Corals grow rings, just like trees. Each ring shows one year of growth. The Great Barrier Reef is about 20,000 years old!

weird but true!

To stay safe, some coral polyps build hard skeletons around their soft bodies. Hard corals like these live in colonies. As generations of skeletons stack up, they form a coral reef. Over hundreds or thousands of years, these reefs grow into massive ocean ecosystems.

Word to Know

ECOSYSTEM: All living and nonliving things that interact in one area

corals

The male pufferfish uses his body to make peaks and valleys in the sand.

A tiny male pufferfish is another busy builder. For about 10 days, he makes patterns with his fins on the sandy ocean floor. He adds corals and shells as decoration. This creates a fancy round nest to attract females.

Decorator crabs have little spikes on their outer skeletons. Pieces of sponges, shells, and seaweed stick to the spikes. Once the crab's body is covered, it blends in with the surroundings.

soft coral decorator crab

Decorator crabs outgrow their hard outer skeleton and grow a new one. Each time, they reuse pieces they have taken off their old shell to redecorate the new one.

weird but true!

Creature Comforts

Two chimpanzees relax in a nest.

Usually, animals build things that help them survive. But for great apes it's more than that. They want comfort!

During the day, apes often build nests on the ground for napping.

An orangutan holds her baby close in their treetop nest.

But at night, they usually build nests high up in the trees. This keeps them safe from predators. The apes start with a bottom layer of sturdy branches. Then they weave a layer of thinner sticks. Finally, they top it off with a comfy layer of leaves.

A bagworm moth caterpillar builds a home to live in. Some bagworm moths stack tiny sticks to make a nest like a log cabin.

Animal architects are everywhere—on land, in the sea, underground, and up in trees. Take a look around your neighborhood. You might be surprised at what you see!

A bagworm moth caterpillar carries its home on its back.

QUIZ WHIZ

How much do you know about animal architects? After reading this book, probably a lot! Take this quiz and find out.

Answers are at the bottom of page 45.

1

What do a large beaver dam in Canada and the Great Barrier Reef have in common?

A. Both are made of wood.
B. Both are in North America.
C. Both can be seen from space.
D. Both are 20,000 years old.

2

An orb spiderweb is shaped like a _____.

A. square
B. circle
C. triangle
D. rectangle

What do Australian weaver ant larvae squirt out to hold a nest together?

A. silk
B. saliva
C. spit
D. poop

3

4

Compass termite mounds always point _____.

A. north
B. south
C. east
D. west

5

How many sides does each cell in a honeycomb have?

A. two
B. four
C. six
D. eight

6

Which of these animals builds a nest?

A. garden spider
B. coral polyp
C. decorator crab
D. great ape

7

Which animal architects have spinnerets?

A. ants
B. termites
C. spiders
D. birds

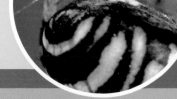

Glossary

ARCHITECT: The designer or creator of something, usually a structure like a building or a bridge

LARVAE: The newly hatched forms of some insects. Larvae don't look like the adults.

NECTAR: The sweet, sticky liquid formed in flowers

POLLEN: A yellow powder made by flowers

PREDATOR: An animal that hunts and eats other animals

COLONY: A group of one kind of plant or animal that lives together

ECOSYSTEM: All living and nonliving things that interact in one area

NYMPH: A newly hatched insect that looks like a tiny adult

ORB: Circular or shaped like a globe

PREY: An animal that is hunted and eaten by another animal

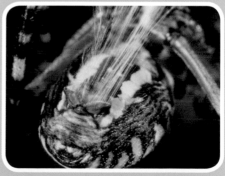

SPINNERET: A small, silk-making part of a spider

Index